Prepper's Medicine Kit:

First Aid Skills and Medications For Your Survival Medicine Kit

Disclamer: All photos used in this book, including the cover photo were made available under a Attribution–NonCommercial–ShareAlike 2.0 Generic and sourced from Flickr

Table of Contents

Introduction

Imagine the scene:

You are out in the countryside enjoying the sun when all of a sudden you hear an explosion up ahead. If an explosion seems unrealistic think of a car crash. You rush over, ensuring the area is free from danger before you enter.

You can see 3 casualties:

- A woman screaming with her arm clearly broken

- An unconscious man who does not look in a good way

- A man wandering around acting erratically in shock

Who do you treat first?

This is the important question when it comes to a situation with multiple casualties and what you do next can mean the difference between somebody dying and somebody staying alive. This is called triage and it is one of the most important lessons in first aid. In the scenario above, you would first look at the unconscious man and check if he is breathing.

If the screaming woman is indeed screaming then it means she is alive and responsive. You also need to ensure the man in shock will not come over to you and do more harm.

Offer strong comforting and encouragement. Tell him everything is going to be ok and that he needs to sit down and have a sweet drink if that is available. Then you can begin to splint the arm of the girl and give her painkillers if necessary.

The point of the above example is that you can know as many first aid tips as you want; the most important thing is to assess the casualties first and prioritize them in order of severity. You are unlikely to come across the situation above but remember the person screaming is the most responsive.

This book will look at tips and tricks for you to treat injuries of varying sizes and severity. We will look at ways you can treat yourself and others with a view of getting professional medical attention in the very near future. Finally we can look at what you might need in your very own personalized first aid kit.

Chapter 1 – Basic injuries – Treatment and Prevention

We need to treat basic wounds and injuries as soon as they occur. If we leave something untreated, it might become infected or exacerbated, which could mean a small injury turns into a large one. If we allow smaller injuries to get worse, it might affect our ability to stay mobile and effective.

A small cut that is left untreated might turn septic or gangrenous and need serious treatment. This might be the worst-case-scenario but it can happen. Look after the smaller wounds and issues before they become major ones.

1. Clean a minor wound.

First ensure your hands are clean; treating a wound with dirty hands might be worse than doing nothing at all. Use antibacterial soap and water to ensure you will not infect your patient. Apply pressure with a clean, sterile cloth until the bleeding has stopped.

Wash the wound to get out any dirt or debris and reapply pressure and elevate if it starts to bleed again. Once the wound is clean and clotted, apply antiseptic cream and a clean, sterile bandage to the affected area. Most basic first aid courses will teach you how to look after a basic wound and bandage it so that the bandage stays in place.

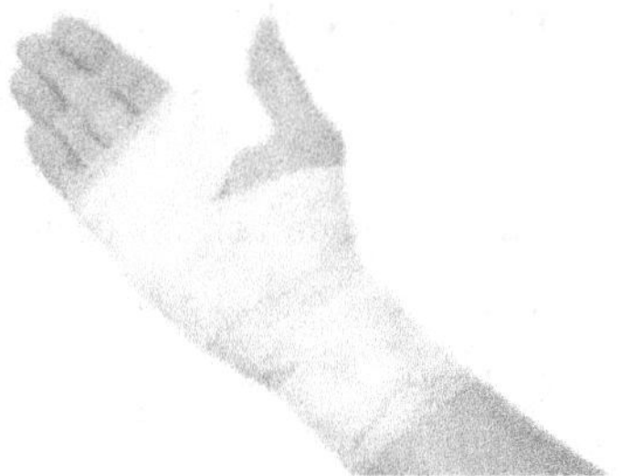

2. Stop chaffing and treated chaffed legs

This might not sound so serious but any soldier who has marched for many miles can tell you how serious this can get. The inside of our legs or our backs can rub in a serious way. If we allow this to continue, we won't be able to move anywhere which might be a serious issue.

The best way to stop chaffing in between our legs is to use cycling shorts or outdoor underwear that will allow for friction and not harm our skin. If we are carrying packs, we should use similar clothing on our torso to avoid blisters and rubbing.

If chaffing occurs, apply skin healing cream such as Savlon as soon as it happens and especially overnight when our skin is trying to heal. Keep the area clean and change out of sweaty clothes as soon as possible. Vaseline and lubricant can be a temporary measure.

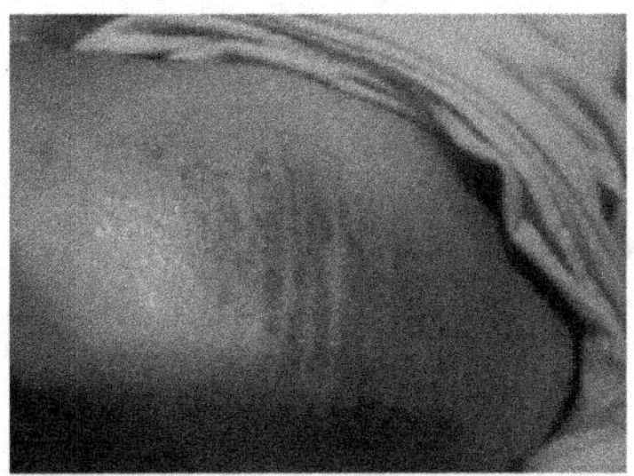

3. Sunburn – treatment and prevention

Sun burn can be a major issue for anyone spending time outside. For preppers and people on the move, sunburn can be a major problem and cause severe pain and discomfort for anyone suffering from it. Fortunately, there is a simple preventative measure that we can take; sunscreen.

Carry Factor 50 to prevent sunburn; don't worry about your tan, worry about your skin. The biggest cause of sunburn is usually people thinking they have tough skin and they don't need sun cream; use it anyway because sunburn can be a mega problem if you get it bad.

Treatment of sunburn involves keeping the affected area covered and using specialist creams that will heal the skin. In the military, soldiers can be charged if they get sunburn as it is always preventable; if you go man-down, you become a liability as you comrades and fellow preppers will have to carry your kit and possibly you.

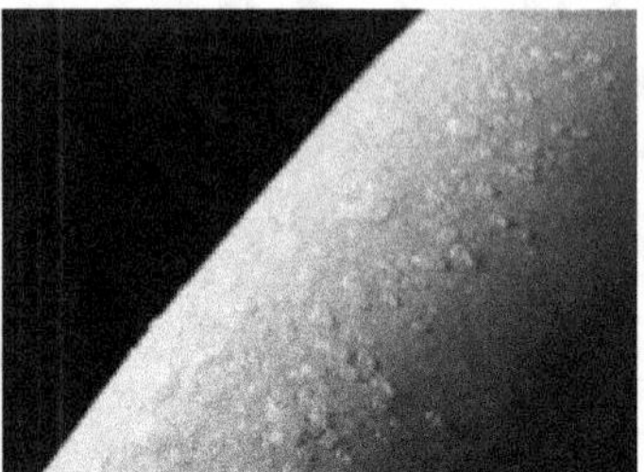

4. Sprains, bumps, blisters and bruises

There is a wide range of minor injuries that can occur whilst out in the wilderness. You first aid kits should be equipped for any eventuality and we will look at what you need to include in the final chapter. If you suffer a trip or fall and injure a limb, you need to assess whether the bone is broken or not. Broken bones might need setting and splinting, depending on the severity and how far away professional help is.

You should feel the limb and attempt movement. If you can move it; you can pretty much rule out a broken bone. Sprains are very common and although they might hurt, support, bandaging and rest will assist in the recovery. There isn't really a lot we can do with bruises; if they happen, they happen and as long as the skin isn't broken, just keep an eye on it to ensure the situation does not deteriorate.

Feet are one of the most important parts of your body; without them, you are going nowhere on feet and this can leave you vulnerable. Hiking long distance can create friction in your boots which will cause blisters. Ensure you clean the wound when you can and apply antiseptic cream to reduce the risk of infection.

Wash your feet and use talcum powder to keep them dry; wet feet can cause trench foot.

You should also ensure that you are using appropriate footwear; travelling long distances over difficult terrain with insufficient footwear can dramatically increase the risk of sprains and ankle injuries

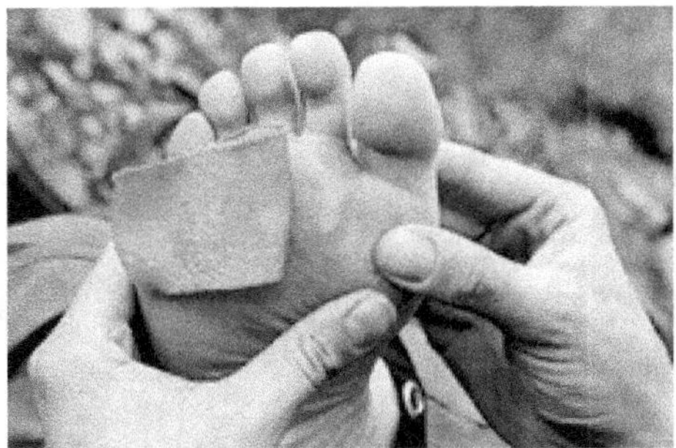

Chapter 2 – Broken bones – Splinting and Recovery

Accidents can happen anywhere, but even more so when out in the wilderness. You may be travelling over harsh terrain, often in low light and it can be difficult to completely avoid injury/ If the worst case scenario occurs and you or one of your party take a fall or trip and break a bone, you need to know what to do in order to stabilize, support and fix the injury until you can get help from a doctor.

1. Assess the situation

When you one of your group has a trip, fall or any other type of accident that might result in broken bones, the first thing you need to do is to assess the situation. Don't move the casualty unless it is unsafe to remain in the current location. Check for other injuries or shock; quite often casualties have been treated for broken bones when bigger problems were left unnoticed.

Check the rest of the body for any wounds and injuries that may happen to be more serious than a broken bone. Next you need to check if the patient is going into shock; check if the skin has gone pale and clammy, check vital signs and responses. If the patient is going into shock you should try and elevate their legs if possible, keep them warm and get a sugary drink into them to help. Rapid shallow breathing is also a big indicator of shock.

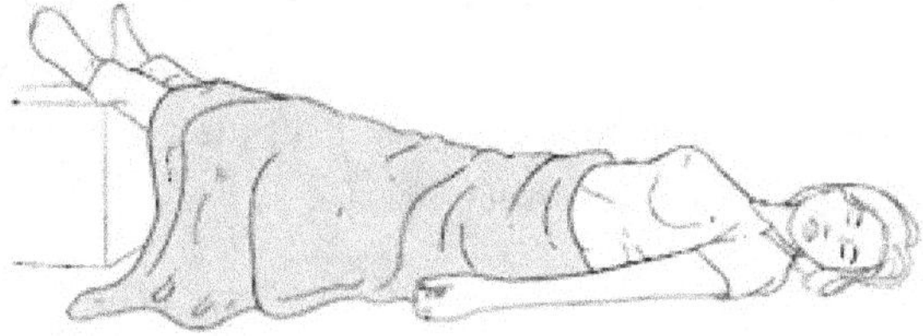

2. Assess the broken bone

There are several different types of break that can occur but as a first-aider without professional equipment, you wouldn't be expected to know them all. The graph below shows the main types of fracture that can occur to a bone. The type of fracture can affect what you need to do next.

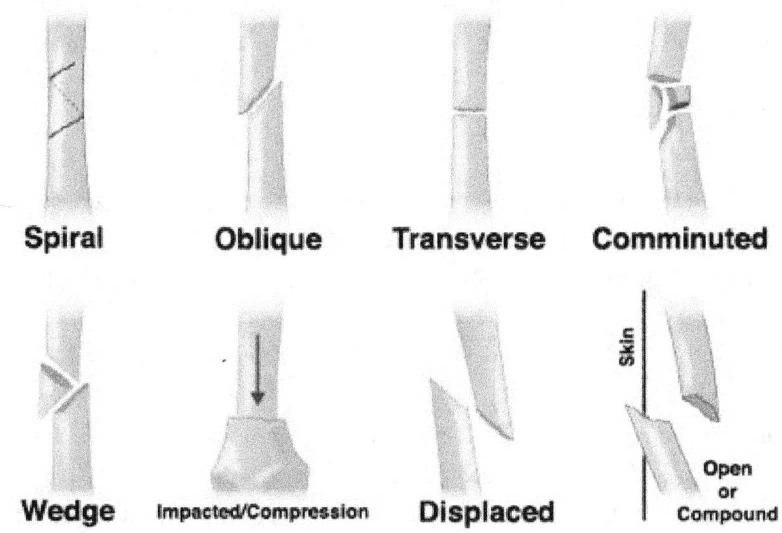

An open fracture is probably the most difficult to deal with because the bone is puncturing the skin and you will have to deal with a hysteric patient, blood loss and infection. The others will be difficult to diagnose without the use of x-ray equipment, which usually isn't on hand in the wilderness, so you deal with it as best you can.

3. Splint the broken limb

The type of bone you are dealing with will also dictate what kind of splint set-up you will need to use. A broken leg is going to need a different splint to a broken hand.

First let's discuss how to deal with an open fracture. This means that the bone has broken severely and is protruding from the skin. The most important thing to remember is not to pull anything out and don't push anything back in. As gruesome as it sounds, stem the bleeding, clean the wound and bandage around the broken bone.

If you need to move somewhere and emergency services cannot get to you, you will need to splint the limb and move location. For demonstration purposes, we will discuss how to splint a broken arm; the same principles can be applied to other limbs.

There are many ways to do it but the principle always stays the same; you are securing the arm so it cannot move and cause further damage. If the arm at a misshapen angle, that cannot be splinted, make a firm movement to bring the limb to the front of the body. To splint the arm you will need something straight, strong and arm's length.

A small but thick branch should do the trick. Strap it to the arm tightly, but not too tight that it restricts blood flow. Put the splint into a sling for extra protect against movement.

4. Recovery and further treatment

Splinting won't heal the arm and the patient will need to seek medical assistance from a professional from a doctor in order to recover correctly.

Broken bones can be extremely painful and splinting is designed to limit movement in order to reduce pain and prevent further damage. It is not a treatment; purely an action to prevent further damage. Only a medical professional can give advice on long term treatment.

Depending on what bone you need to splint, will depend on the next step. A patient with a broken arm can be splinted and then leave the location on foot. A patient with a splinted leg will need to be carried on a stretcher.

Make a stretcher of poles and blankets.

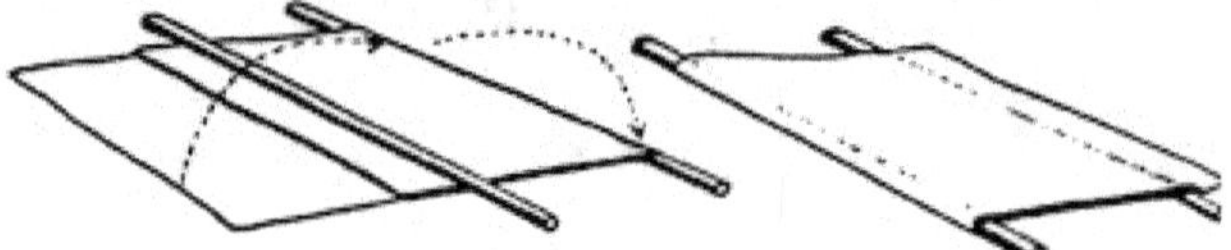

Chapter 3 – Trauma and shock – Strategies and Treatment

Accidents can and will happen when out in the wilderness; it's your job to deal with them when they happen. Not all accidents will be obvious ones; yes there might be broken bones and bumps and bruises, but sometimes the patient will go into shock which can be a dangerous thing. There are several illnesses and incidents that can cause someone to go into shock and if the patient is not treated quickly, severe issues can arise which might lead to death.

1. How to tell if someone has gone into shock:

If someone has gone into shock, depending on the type of shock, they will exhibit some of the following symptoms. The most common to look out for is the rapid shallow breathing and pale, clammy skin.

- **Quick reduction in blood pressure**

- **Rapid, weak, or absent pulse**

- **Irregular heart rate**

- **Confusion and erratic behavior**

- **Pale, clammy skin**

- **Quick and shallow breathing**

- **Anxiety**

- **Lightheadedness and dizziness**

- **Chest pains**

- **Feeling sick**

- **Dehydration**

- **Very low blood sugar**

- **Droopy eyes**

- **Fever**

- **Swollen Face**

2. What can cause shock?

There are many things that can cause a person to go into shock. The body does this because it blood is not reaching the organs and it goes into self-defense mode. Going into shock is a sign that the body is slowly shutting down and without treatment, the patient can die. These are some of the reasons that might cause somebody to go into shock:

- Catastrophic blood loss

- Severe dehydration

- Extreme allergic reaction

- Reduction in blood pressure

- Heart failure – Heart attack

- Nerve or spinal damage

- Blood infections

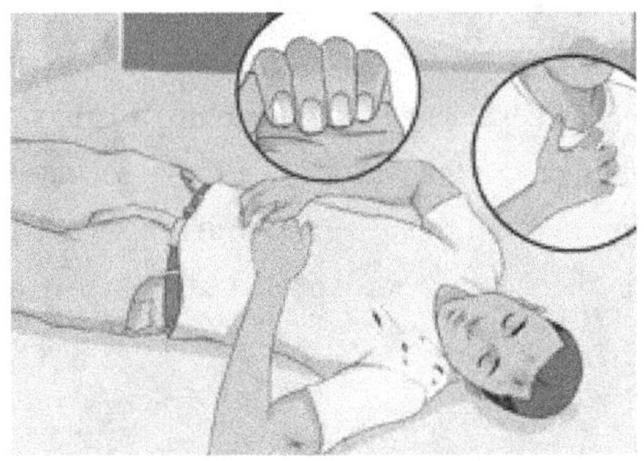

3. Treatment of someone in shock

If you come across someone in shock, your main aim is to provide lifesaving treatment and then diagnose what caused the shock. The first thing to do is to ensure they are lying on their back, if possible.

If there are no broken bones or severe leg injuries, elevate the legs at least 30cm from the ground to improve circulation.

This will improve the flow of blood to the vital organs and get the blood to where it needs to go. Make sure the patient is warm and covered whilst treating any wounds that might need to be treated. You can move the head sideways, if you suspect that there is no spinal or neck damage.

4. Types of shock and further treatment

A full recovery from shock is completely achievable, depending on the treatment given and the speed of application. This is one of the reasons that triage becomes important and we need to assess the injuries and treat them in order of severity. Emergency services must be called immediately when you discover someone going into shock.

Some of the different types of shock:

- **Anaphylactic Shock – Can be caused by allergies**

- **Cardiogenic Shock – Heart damage**

- **Septic Shock – Blood poisoning**

- **Hypovolemic Shock – Blood loss**

Once the patient is stabilized, professionals will try to determine what caused the shock. This can be done via blood tests, scans and x-rays to examine the body.

Preventing shock from happening is the best way to treat it. Stay hydrated, especially in warm climates, wear the proper footwear and clothing to protect yourself and carry the correct medical equipment to deal with an injury quickly.

Chapter 4 – Serious injuries – Worst case scenario

We should always be prepared for the worst case scenario. Some cuts will not stop bleeding with a bandage and might need something extra. Some wounds are not what we think and sometimes we might have to be resourceful if we are going to save our patients life.

Here are some other serious conditions that might happen to you and how you can deal with them. Remember that you should always call emergencies services when possible and they can guide you through emergency treatment of you patient. You should be resourceful and confident but you should not take risks with anybody's life.

1. Frostbite

Frostbite happens when parts of the body start to freeze. This usually occurs to fingers and toes because they are furthest from the heart. You will notices hardening of the skin and a change in color.

They might go gangrenous if left untreated and the patient could lose their fingers or toes. You should catch frostbite before it gets this far and as soon as you seen swelling or discoloration, seek treatment.

To treat frostbite, encourage the patient to put their fingers inside their armpits where it will be warm.

Bring the patient inside and out of the cold if you can. Remove constrictive rings or clothing if possible and soak the affected area in warm, not hot, water. Raise the limbs to reduce swelling and seek professional medical assistance.

Do not try to thaw out frostbite that is in a late stage when medical assistance is not available or you might exacerbate the situation and cause the loss of limbs. You can administer painkillers as the patient is likely to be in severe pain, but do not give them alcohol. A patient suffering from frostbite of the toes should not be made to walk anywhere.

2. Catastrophic bleeds

Sometimes an injury will occur where the bleeding just will not stop, not matter how many bandages you go through or how much pressure is applied.

The patient is in grave danger when this happens and you should contact emergency services immediately. If you cannot contact anyone, there are certain procedures that can be done to improve the chances of survival.

For Catastrophic bleeds on the limbs, and this can also mean the loss of the limb in the worst case scenario, a tourniquet can be applied. Many medical experts have doubted the use of the tourniquet as it can mean that the limb dies and amputation is needed.

A tourniquet does not mean amputation is a guarantee but it does improve the chances that the patient will lose the limb; it might save their life though. A tourniquet means using material to tighten around the limb, above the wound, in order to restrict the blood flow to the limb and to stop the bleeding. Military personnel carry tourniquets but they are an absolute last resort.

Once the tourniquet is applied, the limb should be raised and professional medical help should be sought to loosen the tourniquet gradually. Tourniquets have been around since Roman times in order to stop the limb from bleeding during an amputation. They should only be used as a last resort.

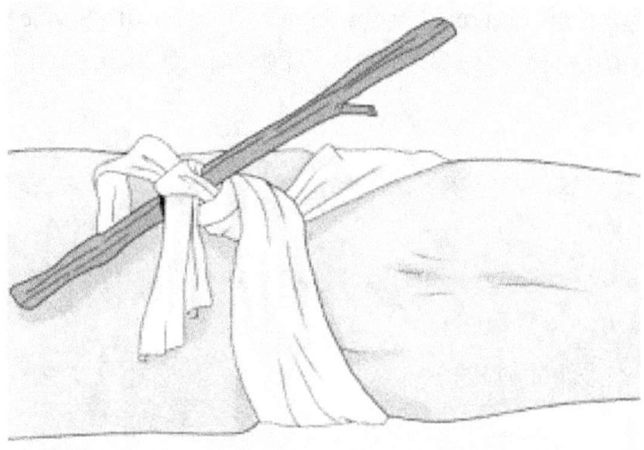

Technology has evolved rapidly and there are better methods than using tourniquets to stop severe bleeds. QuikClot is a product made from volcanic ash that immediately stops bleeds.

It does come with other dangers such as burning of the skin and getting it in your eyes which can blind you, meaning it should be used in an emergency situation only. QuikClot have also developed gauze that does the same job without the risks and is available to the public so you should consider purchasing this for you first aid kit.

3. CPR

Cardiopulmonary Resuscitation goes beyond first aid. CPR is resuscitating a patient whose breathing or heartbeat has stopped. It can occur after drowning or a heart attack and your response can mean life or death for the patient. We have all seen CPR in the movies or the medical television dramas, but the reality can be far different from Hollywood.

The below is how the doctors and professionals from the National Health Service describe the best way to give CPR to a patient.

Without rescue breaths:

Put the palm of your hand on the breastbone of the patient's chest. Then put your other hand over than one and interlock fingers

Place yourself above the patient and at a steady angle and prepare for physical exertion.

You will need to use you full body weight and not just your arms, pressing straight down by around 6cm (2-2.5 inches) on the chest of the patient.

You should keep your hands on their chest, release the compression, and allow the chest of the patient to come back to normal.

Repeat these actions, called compressions, at a rate of 100 to 120 times per minute until emergency services arrive, or until you physically cannot do it any longer.

With Rescue Breaths:

Adults

Put the palm of your hand on the breastbone of the patient's chest. Then put your other hand over than one and interlock fingers

Place yourself above the patient and at a steady angle and prepare for physical exertion.

You will need to use you full body weight and not just your arms, pressing straight down by around 6cm (2-2.5 inches) on the chest of the patient.

You should keep your hands on their chest, release the compression, and allow the chest of the patient to come back to normal.

Once you have completed 30 chest compressions, give two rescue breaths.

Slant the patients head gently and raise the chin with 2 fingers. Pinch the patients nose and seal your mouth over theirs. Blow steadily for a second until you see the chest rise and then fall when you release.

Repeat with the 2 / 30 routine until emergency services arrive, or until you physically cannot do it any longer.

Children over one year old

Place one hand on the forehead of the child and gently tilt back. Remove any debris from the mouth or nose. Pinch the nose and give 5 rescue breaths, watching for the rise and fall of the chest.

Put a firm hand on the center of the chest and push down by roughly 5cm or 2 inches. You should not push down any further but you do need to reach this depth.

Place the heel of one hand on the center of their chest and push down by 5cm (about two inches), which is approximately one-third of the chest diameter. The quality (depth) of chest compressions is very important. Use two hands if you can't achieve a depth of 5cm using one hand.

Repeat with the 2 / 30 routine until emergency services arrive, or until you physically cannot do it any longer.

Infants under one year old

Try to open the patient's airway by putting a hand on the forehead and tilting it back whilst having one hand raising the chin. Remove any debris from the mouth or nose. Pinch the nose and give 5 rescue breaths, watching for the rise and fall of the chest.

Put 2 fingers in the center of the chest and push down by around 4cm or an inch and a half. If you cannot push down far enough with fingers then use the palm of your hand.

Continue with compressions at a rate of 100 to 120 per minute and give 2 rescue breaths every 30 compressions.

Repeat with the 2 / 30 routine until emergency services arrive, or until you physically cannot do it any longer.

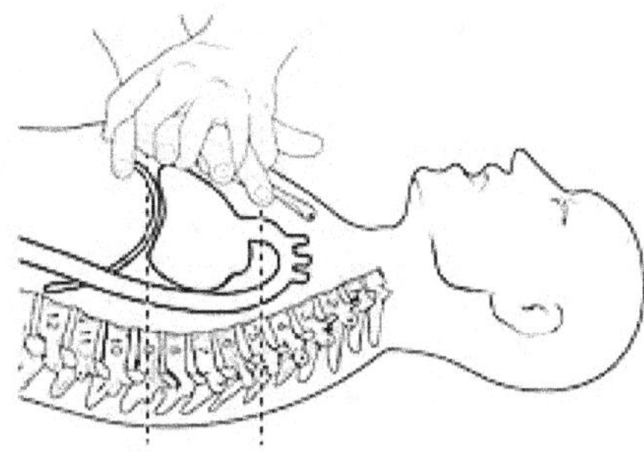

4. Choking

Choking can occur to even healthy individuals and can cause death or loss of consciousness very quickly if not treated quickly. The aim is dislodge whatever is blocking the airway and to get rid of it.

To treat a choking patient, follow these steps:

1. **Cough it out**

Encourage the person to cough

2. **Slap it out**

Administer up to five sharp back blows to the patients back

3. **Squeeze it out**

If over one year old: give up to five abdominal thrusts

If the patient is under one year old: give up to five chest thrusts

If that doesn't work, call for the emergency services.

Choking can be a killer if you do not treat it quickly as the patient will lose consciousness when the oxygen stops going into the lungs. You should learn the warning signs of someone choking and practice the maneuvers, before you need to use the skill in real life. The quicker you treat this condition, the less long term damage might be caused.

1 GIVE 5 BACK BLOWS
Adult:
Child:
Infant:

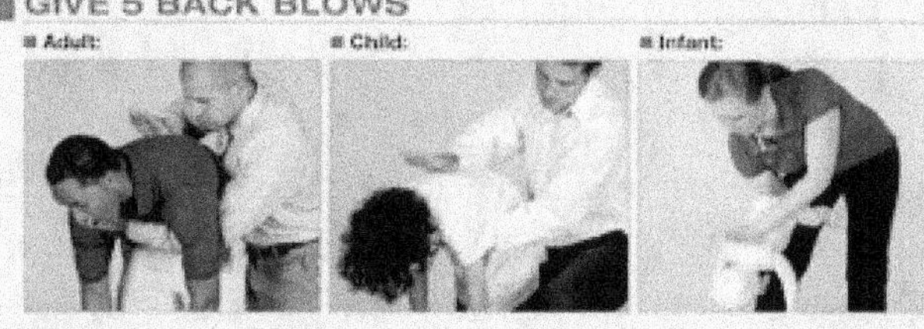

2 GIVE 5 ABDOMINAL THRUSTS
Adult:
Child:
Infant: (chest thrusts for infant)

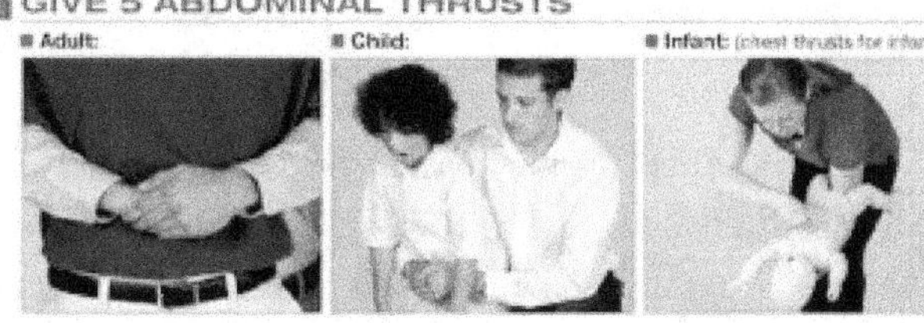

Chapter 5 – What to include in your kit

Experienced preppers and people who spend a great deal of time in the wilderness will personalize their kit through experience and they will know what to include. You will often find that as new technology becomes available, you can replace parts of your kit for upgraded equipment.

You can buy first aid kits for a variety of situations; some are more suitable for the office and some are more suitable for the wilderness. In order to personalize your kit, here is a list of equipment that you might need to treat the injuries and conditions that we discussed previously. As time goes by, you can work out what you will need yourself but here is a good starting guide.

1. **Basic injuries**

- Sterile bandages of varying size and shapes for different parts of the body

- Disposable gloves – Sterile – Multiple pairs

- Hand sanitizer

- Tweezers to remove debris from a cut

- Plasters / Band-Aids - Waterproof

- Antiseptic cream – High quality cream

- Skin healing cream – Savlon

- Gauze to clean wounds - Sterile

- Cream for burns and blisters

- Tape to secure bandages and scissors

- Eye wash solution and eye patches

- First aid manual

- Insect repellant (location depending)

- Factor 50 suntan lotion for emergencies (location depending)

- Aspiring / Paracetamol / Ibuprofen

- Laxatives / diarrhea tablets

- Morphine (Depending on the law in your area)

2. **Broken bones**

- Materials for splinting

- Bandages – sterile

- Sling

- Stretchers – a poncho can double as shelter and a stretcher

- Painkillers – Morphine if available

- First Aid manual – clear and concise

3. **Shock and Trauma**

- Silver foil blankets

- First Aid manual – clear and concise

- Antihistamines

4. **Serious injuries**

- Tourniquet for catastrophic bleeding

- QuikClot – Available online

- Military grade field dressings.

- Sterile needle and surgical thread

- Morphine if legal

- Whistle to get attention

As we mentioned previously, you can personalize your kit as much as you wish and the terrain you will be going into can often dictate what kind of kit you will need.

The most important thing to note when packing and preparing your first aid kit is to pack with the environment in mind. Prepare for where you will be going and know what you might encounter on the way.

Conclusion

The guidelines written in this booklet are intended to give assistance in the best possible procedures in an emergency situation. The best possible course of action is always to call the emergency services as quickly as possible and follow the advice when over the phone.

The operators are trained to verbally guide you on best practices and they are trained to deal with the situation far better than someone who read a few books. Trust in the emergency services and get them involved as soon as an issue has occurred.

We have tried to look at issues from the viewpoint that you may not have battery on your phone, or for any other reason, emergency services cannot be reached. In this case, your actions in the first few minutes are extremely important.

As a prepper, you should be preparing for the worst and having an efficient first aid kit in your kit is one of the most important parts of your grab-bag. A small injury in the field can turn into a major injury if it is not treated quickly and effectively.

You will also need to pack for a wide range of injuries such as heat and cold injuries, as well as broken bones and bleeding. Knowing the basics can mean the difference between saving someone's life and watching them die. A small cut in the wilderness can quickly turn septic and cause major issues unless you treat it quickly and thoroughly.

It is advisable to take part in professionally run first aid courses so that you can practice you first aid skills before you need to use them. You can find great courses online that are run by medical professionals who will instruct you in the best ways to help a casualty.

Techniques and best practices will often change, depending on studies and tests performed by professionals. The best way to stay up to date on the latest advances is to take regular first aid courses run by the professionals.

There are a million different types of incident that might occur whilst out in the field. Preparing for all of them is impossible, so you should be resourceful when it comes to creating a first aid kit. You should create small, concise booklets with all the possible injuries that you might encounter and have it laminated to protect against the environment. In the event of an emergency, when your mind might be elsewhere, you can always refer to the booklet.

In this booklet we have looked at the most common types of injuries that might occur when out in the field. Bleeding, broken bones and shock can all happen extremely suddenly and it might be up to you to save your own life or someone else's. You should be prepared to do whatever is needed, even if the task is gruesome or unpleasant. You should hope for the best but prepare for the worst.

www.ingramcontent.com/pod-product-compliance
Lightning Source LLC
Chambersburg PA
CBHW070102260726
48658CB00002B/959